Savvy

Custom Confections

BAKING BLISS!

BAKED DESSERTS TO MAKE AND DEVOUR

by Jen Besel

CAPSTONE PRESS
a capstone imprint

Savvy Books are published by Capstone Press,
1710 Roe Crest Drive, North Mankato, Minnesota 56003
www.capstonepub.com

Library of Congress Cataloging-in-Publication Data
Besel, Jennifer M., author.
Baking bliss!: baked desserts to make and devour / by Jen Besel.
pages cm. – (Savvy. Custom confections.)
Summary: "Step-by-step instructions teach readers how to bake mouthwatering desserts, including
cakes, cupcakes, cookies, and more" – Provided by publisher.
Audience: Age 9-13.
Audience: Grade 4 to 6.
Includes bibliographical references and index.
ISBN 978-1-4914-0859-9 (library binding)
1. Cake–Juvenile literature. 2. Cookies–Juvenile literature. 3. Cupcakes–Juvenile literature.
4. Baking–Juvenile literature.
I. Title.
TX771.B475 2015
641.8'653–dc23   2014001836

Editorial Credits
Ashlee Suker, designer; Sarah Schuette, photo stylist; Marcy Morin, scheduler;
Danielle Ceminsky, production specialist

Photo Credits
All images by Capstone Studio: Karon Dubke

Printed in the United States of America in North Mankato, Minnesota.
032014   008087CGF14

TABLE of CONTENTS

MOUTHWATERING DESSERTS
... Baked by You!

Get out your tools. Preheat the oven. And get ready! You're about to bake up treats that look as good as they taste. Want to make some mouthwatering cookies? Need an elegant cake for that special event? Or do you just want to serve something unexpected? You've come to the right place.

You don't need to be a professional baker to make custom desserts. With a few ingredients and some simple steps, you can create your own delicious treats. And you won't have to spend days in the kitchen to do it. (But you can let your guests think you did.)

So jump right in. What custom confection will you bake first?

Convert It

The recipes in this book use U. S. measurements.
If you need metric measurements, here's a
handy conversion guide.

United States	Metric
¼ teaspoon	1.2 mL
½ teaspoon	2.5 mL
1 teaspoon	5 mL
1 tablespoon	15 mL
¼ cup	60 mL
⅓ cup	80 mL
½ cup	120 mL
⅔ cup	160 mL
¾ cup	175 mL
1 cup	240 mL
1 quart	1 liter
1 ounce	30 grams
2 ounces	55 grams
4 ounces	110 grams
½ pound	225 grams
1 pound	455 grams

Fahrenheit	Celsius
200°	90°
300°	140°
325°	160°
350°	180°
375°	190°
400°	200°
425°	220°
450°	230°

TOOLS

You'll need some kitchen tools to create mouthwatering treats. But don't worry. You probably have most of these in your kitchen already.

cookie cutters {1}
cake stands or serving platters {2}
fine sieve {3}
cake boards {4}
cutting board {5}
pastry scraper {6}
electric mixer {7}
cake pans {8}
lemon zester {9}
sprinkles {10}
bowls {11}
spoons {12}

muffin tins {13}
cupcake liners {14}
baking sheets {15}
cooling rack {16}
piping bags and tips {17}
angel food pan {18}
small basting brush {19}
rolling pin {20}
wax paper {21}
measuring spoons {22}
ramekins {23}
serrated knife {24}

1 teaspoon cream of tartar

1 teaspoon salt

1 teaspoon baking soda

5 cups flour

1 cup granulated sugar

1 cup powdered sugar

1 cup butter, softened

2 eggs

1 cup vegetable oil

1 tablespoon vanilla extract

1 teaspoon almond extract

food coloring

edge royal icing (*See page 44 for recipe.*)

sprinkles and mini candies

HIDDEN PRESENT *Cookies*

These fun cookies are as sweet inside
as they are outside.

1 Gather a large gift-shaped cookie cutter and a small square cutter.
Then find a plastic container that's as tall as the gift cutter. Cover the
inside of the container with plastic wrap. Set the container and cookie
cutters aside.

2 Stir together the cream of tartar, salt, baking soda, and
flour in a large bowl.

3 In another bowl cream together the sugars and butter.
Beat in the eggs, then the oil.

4 Slowly beat the flour mixture into the sugar mixture.
Finally, mix in the vanilla and almond extracts.

5 Split the dough into six balls. Knead food
coloring into each ball. Then split each
colored ball in half.

6 Press one half-ball into the bottom of the
plastic-wrapped container.

7 Press a half-ball of another color into the
container on top of the first. Continue layering
the dough, alternating colors as you go, until
you've put all the dough into the container.

8 Cover the dough with plastic wrap. Then put the
container in the freezer for at least four hours.

continued on next page

9 Preheat the oven to 350°. Take the dough out of the freezer, and lift it out of the container by pulling up on the plastic wrap. Remove the plastic wrap from the dough.

10 Cut the dough into ¼-inch slices.

11 Line a baking sheet with parchment paper. Lay the dough slices on the sheet in rows of three. Bake for 12 minutes.

12 After taking the cookies out of the oven, press the gift-shaped cookie cutter into each slice. But don't lift the shape out just yet.

13 While the cookies are still hot, also use the square cookie cutter to press out the center area of one cookie in each row. Remove the center area and set aside.

}

14 Let the cookies cool. When they are cool, carefully lift them off the baking sheet and remove the excess cookie around the shape. Lay the gift-shaped cookies on your workspace.

15 Put the royal icing in a piping bag. Outline one whole cookie with icing.

16 Lay a cookie with the center cut out on top of the icing. Fill the hole with sprinkles or candies.

17 Outline the filled cookie with icing, and lay another whole cookie on top.

18 Repeat steps 15–17 to finish the rest of the cookies.

19 Pipe royal icing onto the cookies to create bows. Let the icing harden for 30 minutes.

BLACK AND WHITE
Angel Food

Chocolate and orange are a surprising combination. But use the flavors in this layered angel food cake for a heavenly dessert.

1 box angel food cake mix

2 tablespoons +
¾ teaspoon unsweetened
dark cocoa powder

1 teaspoon orange extract,
divided

1 tablespoon + ¼ teaspoon
orange zest

1¼ cups powdered sugar

3 tablespoons milk

1 orange

1 Preheat the oven to 350°.

2 Prepare the cake batter as directed on the package. Pour half the batter into another bowl.

3 Add 2 tablespoons cocoa powder to one bowl of batter. Gently fold the cocoa in.

4 Add ½ teaspoon orange extract and 1 tablespoon orange zest to the other bowl of batter. Gently stir.

5 Pour the chocolate batter into an ungreased angel food cake pan. Pour the orange-flavored batter on top.

Custom Tip

If you're not a fan of oranges, that's OK. Just leave out the orange extract and zest. Then garnish with your favorite fruit.

6 Bake the cake according to package directions. When the cake is finished baking, carefully remove the pan from the oven. Immediately turn the pan upside down and place it on top of an upside-down flower pot or glass. Let the cake cool completely in this position.

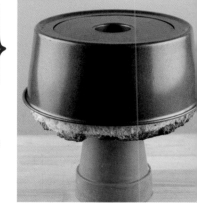

7 Once the cake is cool, set it upright. Loosen the cake from the sides of the pan by running a butter knife around the edges. Place a plate on top of the pan. Then flip the pan and plate together. The cake should sit on the plate when you remove the pan.

8 Pour the powdered sugar into a small bowl. Add the milk, and stir to create a syruplike glaze. Pour half of the glaze into another bowl.

9 Add ½ teaspoon orange extract and ¼ teaspoon orange zest to one bowl of glaze. Stir together. Drizzle the orange glaze over the cake.

10 Add ¾ teaspoon of cocoa to the second bowl of glaze and stir. Add a splash of milk if needed to get a syruplike consistency. Drizzle the chocolate glaze over the cake.

11 Cut the orange into thin slices and arrange on top.

CHECKERBOARD
Cake

Roses are a sweet way to decorate any cake.
But don't let the beauty stop there. Bake a cake
with a gorgeous checkerboard of color that's sure
to surprise and delight.

1 box white cake mix

1 box chocolate cake mix

food coloring

vanilla buttercream frosting, colored as you wish *(See page 46 for the recipe.)*

1 Mix the box of white cake mix according to package directions. Divide the batter into two bowls.

2 Mix up the box of chocolate cake mix according to package directions. Pour half the batter into another bowl, and save it for another use.

3 Add food coloring to one bowl of white batter. Stir until the color is blended. }

4 Cover the insides of three round baking pans with nonstick cooking spray. Pour each bowl of batter into a greased pan. Bake the cakes according to package directions.

5 Allow the cakes to cool to room temperature.

6 Wrap each cake in two layers of plastic wrap. Put them in the refrigerator for at least one hour.

7 Remove the cakes from the refrigerator and unwrap them.

8 Center a plastic lid from an oatmeal container (or a round object of similar size) on one of the cakes. Cut around the lid. Then carefully remove the center piece of cake. }

continued on next page

9 Repeat step 8 with the other two cakes.

10 Lay one of the outside rings of cake on a serving plate or cake board. Spread a thin layer of frosting around the inside ring. Then put an inside circle of a different color cake in the hole.

11 Spread a layer of frosting over the cake layer you made in step 10. Then lay another outside cake ring on top of the first. Frost inside the ring and fill with a different color center circle.

12 Repeat step 11 with the last two pieces of cake.

13 Spread a thin layer of buttercream frosting over the entire cake.

14 Fill a piping bag with frosting. Pipe large roses all around the side of the cake. Then do the same on the top. (For piping tips, go to page 47.)

15 Fill in the empty areas between the roses with a swoop of frosting that goes the same direction as the rose next to it.

10

13

15

MINI APPLE
Cakes

Celebrate autumn or the first day of school with these fun apple-shaped cake balls. They'll make raking leaves or cracking the books just a little bit sweeter.

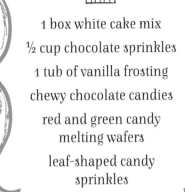

1 box white cake mix
½ cup chocolate sprinkles
1 tub of vanilla frosting
chewy chocolate candies
red and green candy melting wafers
leaf-shaped candy sprinkles

1 Preheat the oven to 350°. Spray a baking pan with nonstick cooking spray. Prepare the cake mix, and bake according to package directions.

2 Let the cake cool completely. Then crumble the cake into a bowl so there are no large pieces. Pour in the chocolate sprinkles.

3 Add frosting to the bowl of cake pieces one spoonful at a time. Mix well after each addition. Your mixture should be a moist dough that you can shape into balls. If it seems too dry and falls apart easily, add more frosting. You'll probably use almost a full tub of frosting.

4 Scoop out 1 tablespoon of cake mixture. Gently shape the mixture into an apple shape. Place the apple on a baking sheet lined with wax paper. Roll the rest of the mixture into little apples. Then refrigerate them overnight.

5 Cut the chewy chocolate candies into thin strips. Roll the strips into tubes to look like apple stems.

6 Melt the red and green candy wafers according to package directions.

7 Dip one end of a lollipop stick into one of the bowls of melted candy. Press the candy-coated end into the flat bottom of an apple. Place the apple back on the baking sheet to let the candy dry while you repeat with the rest.

8 Dip an apple into one color of melted candy. Tap the stick on the bowl to remove any excess candy. Before the candy coating dries, press in a chocolate stem and a leaf-shaped candy. Press the sticks into a foam block to let the apples dry.

9 Repeat step 8 with the rest of the apples. Once the candy coating is completely set, carefully pull the apples off the sticks, if you wish.

SWEETHEART
Cupcakes

Show how much you care with one sweet
and surprising dessert. It's easier to do
than you might think!

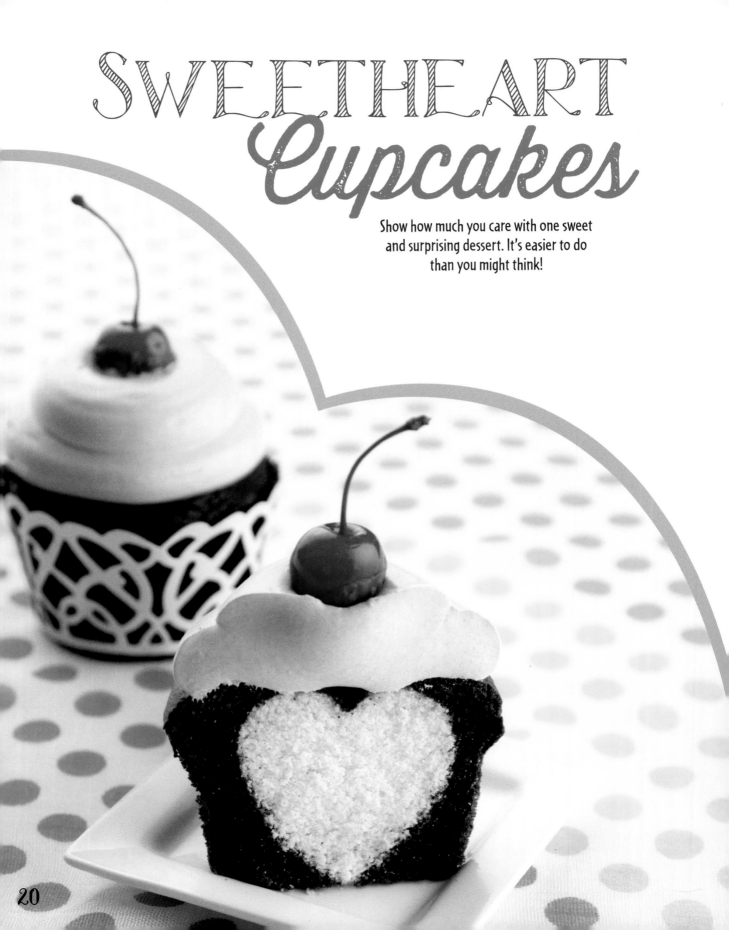

1 box white cake mix

1 box chocolate cake mix

cherry buttercream frosting
(See page 46 for recipe.)

½ cup semisweet
chocolate chips

maraschino cherries

1 Spray an 8-inch square baking pan with nonstick spray. Make the white cake mix according to package directions.

2 Pour 1½ cups of the batter into the greased pan. (Save the rest of the batter for some extra cupcakes or another small cake project.)

3 Bake at 350° for about 20 minutes or until a toothpick inserted into the center comes out clean. Let the cake cool completely.

4 Run a butter knife around the edges of the cake. Lay a cutting board on top of the pan. Carefully turn the board and pan over together. Lift the pan straight up, letting the cake sit on the cutting board.

5 Use a heart-shaped cookie cutter to press hearts out of the cake.

6 Put cupcake liners in a muffin tin.

continued on next page

7 Prepare the chocolate cake mix according to package directions. Pour 2 tablespoons of the chocolate batter into each liner.

8 Gently press a cake heart into the batter in each liner. The bottom of the heart should point down. Cover each heart with a bit more chocolate batter.

9 Bake the cupcakes at 350° for 24 to 26 minutes. When done, let the cupcakes sit in the pan for 10 minutes. Then transfer them to a cooling rack. Let them cool completely before frosting.

10 Fill a piping bag with cherry buttercream frosting. Pipe a generous amount of frosting on top of each cupcake.

11 Put the chocolate chips in a microwave-safe bowl. Melt the chips in the microwave on high for 30 seconds, stopping after 15 seconds to stir.

12 Gently dry the cherries, then dip them into the melted chocolate. Finish each cupcake with a chocolate-covered cherry on top.

PERFECT
Pie Pops

Any food is more fun when it's on a stick!
Turn your favorite pie into a pie pop
that's perfect for any occasion.

2 boxes refrigerated pie
crusts, softened

canned pie filling, any flavor

1 egg, beaten

white sparkling sugar

1. Preheat the oven to 450°. Line two baking sheets with parchment paper.

2. Unroll two pie crusts onto a floured work surface. Use a round cookie cutter to punch out eight circles from each crust. Lay half of the circles on a baking sheet.

3. Press one craft stick or thin dowel into the center of each circle on the baking sheet.

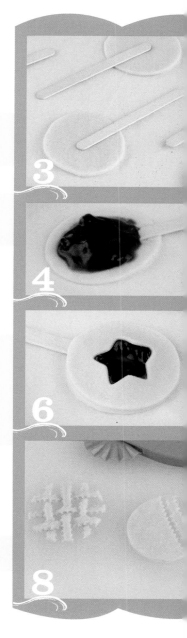

4. Spoon 1 tablespoon pie filling onto each circle. Leave about ½ inch around the edge.

5. Use small shape cookie cutters to punch out shapes from the centers of the circles left on the work surface.

6. Brush the edges of the circles on the baking sheet with egg. Then lay one circle with a cutout shape over each circle on the baking sheet. Gently press the edges together. Then use a fork to make indents around the edges.

7. Repeat steps 2–3 with the other two full crusts.

8. Cut eight of the circles into ¼-inch wide strips.

9. Spoon 1 tablespoon pie filling onto each circle. Then brush the edges of these with egg.

10. Lay three strips over the filling on each circle. Then weave three more strips over and under the first strips. Press the edges together on each pie pop.

11. Brush the tops of all the pie pops with egg. Sprinkle with sparkling sugar.

12. Bake for 10 to 13 minutes or until golden. Let the pies rest on a cooling rack before eating.

PB and J CHEESECAKE Brownies

Turn basic brownies into showstoppers with a cheesecake topping swirled with everyone's favorite combo—peanut butter and jelly.

1 Preheat the oven to 325°. Line a 9x13-inch baking pan with parchment paper, letting some hang over the sides.

2 Make the brownie mix according to package directions. Spread the batter in the pan.

3 Beat the cream cheese, sugar, flour, and vanilla until well blended. Add the sour cream. Then mix in the eggs, one at a time, just until blended.

4 Spread the cream cheese mixture over the brownie batter.

5 Put the peanut butter in a microwave-safe bowl. Melt for 15 to 30 seconds until the peanut butter is a bit runny.

6 Drop spoonfuls of jam and peanut butter on top of the cream cheese. Pull a knife through the cream cheese to swirl the jam and peanut butter.

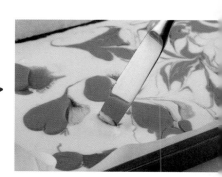

7 Bake for 40 minutes or until the center is almost set.

8 Let the brownies cool completely in the pan. Once they're cool, lift the parchment paper straight up to remove the brownies from the pan. If desired, use cookie cutters to cut shapes out of the brownies. Or you can just cut them into basic squares.

1 box brownie mix

20 ounces cream cheese, softened

½ cup granulated sugar

1½ tablespoons flour

½ tablespoon vanilla extract

½ cup sour cream

2 eggs

1 cup creamy peanut butter

1 cup raspberry jam

BLUEBERRY CHEESECAKE *Tarts*

Make these mouthwatering bites for your next party. The sugar cookie crust, blueberry filling, and cheesecake are a winning combination.

1 Preheat the oven to 325°. Spray a muffin tin with nonstick cooking spray.

2 Roll each precut piece of sugar cookie dough into a ball. Place one ball in each muffin cup.

3 Bake the dough for six to seven minutes or until golden brown. Remove from the oven. Press down the middle of each cookie to form a cup.

4 Beat the cream cheese, condensed milk, egg, and vanilla in a medium bowl until combined.

5 Drop 1 teaspoon of pie filling into each cup. Then pour 2 teaspoons of cream cheese mixture on top to fill each cup.

6 Bake the tarts at 325° for five minutes or until the cheesecake mixture is set.

7 When they're finished baking, carefully pop each tart out of the tin with a spoon. Set the tarts on a cooling rack.

8 When cool, top each tart with blueberry filling or fresh blueberries.

1 package refrigerated precut
sugar cookie dough

1 8-ounce package cream cheese, softened

¾ cup sweetened condensed milk

1 egg

1 teaspoon vanilla extract

blueberry pie filling

fresh blueberries, if desired

Red Velvet Cookies

Combine tasty red velvet cake with a sweet cream cheese filling, and you'll have treats that won't stay in the cookie jar for long.

1 box red velvet cake mix

2 eggs

1/3 cup oil

2 teaspoons vanilla extract, divided

4½ cups powdered sugar, divided

½ cup butter, softened

1 8-ounce package cream cheese, softened

1 Preheat the oven to 375°. Line two baking sheets with parchment paper.

2 Mix the cake mix, eggs, oil, and 1 teaspoon vanilla in a large bowl. The dough will be sticky.

3 Put ½ cup powdered sugar in a separate bowl.

4 Scoop out 1 heaping tablespoon of dough. Drop the dough into the powdered sugar. Completely cover the dough with sugar and roll into a ball. Then put the ball on a baking sheet. Repeat with the rest of the dough. Place each dough ball 3 inches away from other balls.

5 Bake the cookies for seven to 10 minutes. Let them set for two minutes in the pan before setting on a cooling rack.

6 Cream the butter, cream cheese, and 1 teaspoon vanilla in a large bowl. Slowly add 4 cups powdered sugar, mixing until the frosting is smooth.

7 Put the frosting in a piping bag.

8 Turn one cookie upside down. Pipe a generous amount of frosting on the cookie. Press another cookie on top. Repeat with all the cookies.

BOSTON CREAM *Bites*

Make these tasty treats in two sizes—regular and mini. Then guests can choose just how much deliciousness they can handle.

1 Preheat the oven to 350°. Spray a regular-size muffin tin and a mini muffin tin with nonstick spray.

2 Make the cake mix according to package directions.

3 Fill the regular-size cups with ⅓ cup batter. Bake for 18 to 21 minutes or until a toothpick inserted in the center comes out clean.

4 Let the cupcakes sit in the pan for about 15 minutes. Then move them to a cooling rack.

5 Fill each mini cup with 2 tablespoons of batter. Bake at 350° for nine to 11 minutes or until a toothpick inserted in the center comes out clean.

6 Let the cupcakes sit in the pan for about 15 minutes. Then move them to a cooling rack.

7 When both the regular and mini cupcakes are completely cool, cut off the top of each cupcake. Carefully set the tops aside.

1 box yellow cake mix

2 cups cold milk

2 3.4-ounce packages instant
vanilla pudding mix

3 cups whipped topping, thawed

2 cups dark chocolate chips

1½ cups heavy cream

~continued on next page~

8 Beat the milk and pudding together for two minutes. Then gently fold in the whipped topping.

9 Fill a piping bag with the pudding mixture. Pipe a generous amount of pudding mixture on top of each cupcake bottom.

10 Press the cupcake tops back on the cupcakes.

11 Pour the chocolate chips and cream into a small microwave-safe bowl. Heat uncovered for 30 to 60 seconds or until the chips are smooth when stirred.

12 Spoon melted chocolate over the top of each cupcake. Let the chocolate set for at least one hour.

½ cup butter

4 ounces semisweet
baking chocolate

1 cup powdered sugar

2 whole eggs

2 egg yolks

6 tablespoons flour

4 pieces chewy caramel

sea salt

MOLTEN CARAMEL Cake

Ooey, gooey salted caramel steals the show in this delicious take on a traditional lava cake.

1 Preheat the oven to 425°. Spray four custard cups or four cups in a muffin tin with nonstick cooking spray.

2 Put the butter and chocolate in a large microwave-safe bowl. Heat until the butter melts. Then stir until the mixture is smooth.

3 Add the powdered sugar to the chocolate mixture, and stir until smooth. Then stir in the eggs and egg yolks.

4 Pour the flour into the chocolate mixture and stir just until combined.

5 Divide the chocolate mixture among the cups.

6 Cut each caramel piece into four quarters. Press a generous pinch of sea salt into each caramel quarter.

7 Press four salted caramel quarters into the batter in each cup. Make sure the batter covers them.

8 Bake the cups for 12 to 13 minutes or until the sides are set but the center is soft.

9 Let the cakes rest for two minutes. Then turn the cakes out onto plates.

10 Sprinkle the top of each cake with sea salt. Serve right away.

Custom Tip

Here's an easy way to separate an egg. Hold your washed hand palm up over a bowl. Have someone crack an egg into your hand. Let the egg whites drip between your fingers. The yolk will be in your palm.

STAINED GLASS *Cookies*

Brighten up plain old sugar cookies with a stained-glass look. Created with melted hard candies, this will be one kind of glass you won't mind breaking.

38

1 Preheat the oven to 350°. Roll out the cookie dough according to package directions. The dough should be about ¼ inch thick.

2 Use a large cookie cutter to cut out as many shapes from the dough as you can.

3 Use a smaller cookie cutter to punch out a shape inside each larger shape. Remove the small shapes and set aside.

4 Cover a baking sheet with parchment paper. Place the large shapes on the baking sheet.

5 Separate the hard candies by color. Put each color in a separate zip-top bag. Smash the candies into small pieces.

6 Fill the inside hole of each cookie with candy pieces. Fill the holes just up to the top edge. You can use one color or mix colors for a fun effect.

7 Bake the cookies for six to eight minutes or until the candy is melted. Let the cookies cool completely on the pan before removing them.

8 Color the edge royal icing as you wish. Then put it in a piping bag. Pipe icing around the outer edges of the cookies. Let the icing dry for at least one hour.

1 package refrigerator sugar cookie dough

colorful hard candies, unwrapped

food coloring

edge royal icing *(See page 44 for recipe.)*

LAYERED FRUIT *Pastry*

Pile on the sweetness with this delicious and beautiful dessert. Traditionally called a mille-feuille (pronounced mil-FWEE), this delicate confection is sure to please.

2½ cups flour

¾ teaspoon salt

3 sticks cold butter

¾ cup ice-cold water

2 cups whole milk

6 tablespoons granulated sugar

3 tablespoons cornstarch

½ teaspoon banana extract

fresh strawberries, washed and patted dry

fresh blueberries, washed and patted dry

1 Cut the butter into small pieces, and put them in a bowl. Put the bowl in the refrigerator for 10 minutes. Then sift the flour and salt over the butter.

2 Cut the butter into the flour to make a crumbly mixture. }

3 Add a bit of the water to the flour mixture. Mix the water into the flour. Continue adding water and mixing until the mixture becomes a loose dough.

4 Sprinkle flour on a large cutting board. Put the dough on the board.

5 Roll the dough out into a rectangle. Lift one end of the rectangle, and fold the end over so the edge lines up with the middle of the rectangle. Lift and fold the other end over. }

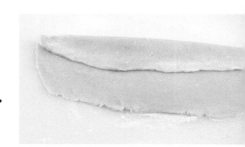

6 Shape the edges of the dough so you have a nice, even rectangle. Then rotate the dough a quarter turn. }

7 Repeat steps 5–6 four more times. By the end, the dough should have several layers, be smooth, and stick together well.

8 Wrap the dough in plastic wrap and put it in the refrigerator for 30 minutes.

9 Repeat steps 5–6 two more times.

continued on next page

10 Preheat the oven to 400°. While the oven is warming, roll out the dough until it's about ½ inch thick.

11 Use cookie cutters to cut out rectangles. Put the rectangles on parchment paper-lined baking sheets. Use a fork to poke the rectangles all over.

12 Lay another piece of parchment paper on top of the dough rectangles. Then gently set an empty baking sheet on top of the paper.

13 Bake the dough for 20 minutes. Remove the top baking sheet and parchment paper. Bake for another five minutes or until golden.

14 Cool the pastries on a wire rack.

15 Mix the milk, sugar, and cornstarch in a large pan. Stir until the sugar is almost dissolved.

16 Put the pan on the stove over medium heat. Bring the mixture to a boil, stirring constantly.

17 Continue stirring as the mixture simmers for three to five minutes. When the mixture becomes very thick, remove the pan from the heat.

18 Stir in the banana extract.

19 Pour the pastry cream mixture into a bowl and cover with plastic wrap. Refrigerate the mixture while you work on step 20.

20 Cut the strawberries into thin slices.

21 Fill a piping bag with pastry cream. Pipe cream onto one of the puff pastries.

22 Arrange a layer of strawberry slices on the cream. Then lay another pastry on top of the strawberries.

23 Pipe cream on the second pastry. Arrange blueberries on top of this layer. Then top with a last piece of pastry.

24 Pipe cream on the top layer. Then arrange strawberries and blueberries on top for a pretty finish.

Royal Icing

2 teaspoons meringue powder
2 tablespoons water
2 to 2½ cups powdered sugar

Edge and flood royal icings are made with the same ingredients. The only difference is how stiff you make the icing. Stiffer edge icing is perfect for creating outlines or decorations that need to hold a shape. Use flood icing to easily cover a large area.

Edge Icing

With an electric mixer on high, blend the ingredients together in a bowl for about four to five minutes. The icing is the right consistency when it forms little peaks that hold their shape. Pour the edge icing into a piping bag with a round tip to create designs or borders.

Flood Icing

Make a batch of edge icing. Then add water ½ teaspoon at a time, blending after each addition. The icing is ready when drips hold their shape for just a moment before they blend back into the icing. Spoon this icing onto a cookie or other dessert. Then use a toothpick or small paintbrush to spread it out.

Tips for Working with Royal Icing

Color

Add food coloring to the icing after you've blended it to the right consistency. Remember, a little goes a long way—so start with just a few drops. You can always add more if you want a darker color.

Taste

You can add flavoring to your icing, if you wish. Just replace all or part of the water with the extract of your choice. Try vanilla, raspberry, or lemon.

Design

If you're planning to cover an entire cookie or other dessert with royal icing, start with a border. Use edge icing to make an outline around the edge of the treat. Let the border dry. Then fill in the shape with flood icing.

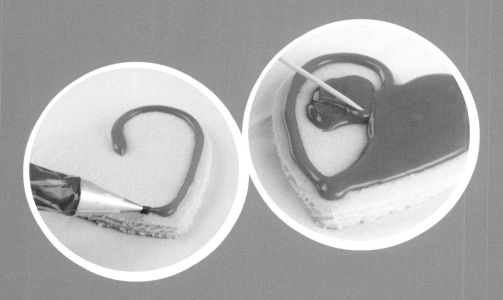

Vanilla Buttercream Frosting

½ cup unsalted butter,
softened
½ teaspoon vanilla extract
2 cups powdered sugar
1–2 tablespoons milk

1. In a large bowl, cream the butter and vanilla until fluffy.

2. Alternate adding sugar and milk until the ingredients are mixed well. The frosting should be thick, creamy, and spreadable. Scrape the sides of the bowl often with a spatula.

Variations

For chocolate frosting, follow the recipe above, and add ¼ cup unsweetened cocoa powder along with the sugar.

For peanut butter frosting, follow the recipe above but leave out the vanilla extract. Add in 1 cup creamy peanut butter and an extra tablespoon of milk.

For cherry frosting, replace the milk with maraschino cherry juice. Replace the vanilla with almond extract.

Piping Tips

To make a rose:

1. Put a 1mm open star tip on the piping bag. Hold the bag straight up from a cake top. Squeeze out a star.

2. Continue squeezing with even pressure, and swirl frosting around the star without lifting the bag up. When the top is covered, stop squeezing and pull the bag straight away from the cake.

To make a cupcake swirl:

1. Put a 1mm open star tip on the piping bag. Hold the bag straight up from a cake top. Squeeze out a star.

2. Continue squeezing with even pressure while lifting the bag slightly. Swirl frosting around the cake until the top is covered.

3. Continue squeezing as you move back to the center of the cupcake. Do another swirl on top of the first. Then stop squeezing and pull the bag straight away from the cupcake.

Glossary

GLAZE (GLAYZ)—a liquid mixture applied to food on which it forms a firm, glossy coating

PARCHMENT PAPER (PARCH-muhnt PAY pur)—paper sold in rolls used for baking

PREHEAT (pre-HEET)—turn an oven on before you use it; it usually takes about 15 minutes to preheat an oven

SIFT (SIFT)—to put through a sifter or a sieve

TART (TART)—an open pie that usually has a sweet filling

Read More

Besel, Jen. *Sweet Tooth!: No-Bake Desserts to Make and Devour.* Custom Confections. North Mankato, Minn.: Capstone Press, 2015.

McKenney, Sally. *Sally's Baking Addiction: Irresistible Cupcakes, Cookies, and Desserts for Your Sweet Tooth Fix.* New York: Race Point Pub., 2014.

Turnbull, Stephanie. *Cool Stuff to Bake.* Cool Stuff. Mankato, Minn.: Smart Apple Media, 2015.

Internet Sites

FactHound offers a safe, fun way to find Internet sites related to this book. All of the sites on FactHound have been researched by our staff.

Here's all you do:

Visit *www.facthound.com*

Type in this code: 9781491408599